TRUE SUCCESS IN A CAREER

The high school student's guide to discovering career satisfaction

A True Success Book from True Colors®

Carolyn Kalil

True Colors, Inc. Publishing
Riverside, California

Our vision at True Colors is to foster positive, healthy, productive communities whose successes flow from the natural dedication of each person. Our powerful, customized "edutainment" workshops, books, workbooks, videos, live shows and events have empowered millions of people during the past twenty years and helped to realize this vision.

True Colors, Inc. Publishing is proud to release **True Success in a Career**, the premier book in our **True Success** series. Written specifically for high school students, this latest offering by noted author and counselor Carolyn Kalil, M.A. guides them in choosing occupations ranging from entry level to professional careers in which they will find true satisfaction. Based upon Don Lowry's True Colors® concept of temperament and personality typing, **True Success in a Career** is designed to be completed in a classroom setting over five to ten weeks. However, it can also be completed as an extracurricular activity by individual students with regular access to career and academic counselors.

We offer this new workbook with the confidence and conviction that it will serve you well, and lead students on a happy and rewarding experience in discovering **True Success in a Career**.

Printed in the U.S.A.
ISBN 1-893320-24-3

Edited by Mike Berry
Book design by Michael "Hoss" Church

TCB-030

Dear Student,

I see many students who are frustrated and discouraged with their attempts to decide on a major or career. I believe part of the problem may be our rather naïve perception that we can do anything if it pays enough money and has enough status.

We are capable of doing almost anything we set our minds to. However, knowledge of our personality preferences or "True Colors" will help us understand why we are not motivated to do just anything.

By nature we are motivated toward certain pursuits and not others. Being aware of our personality preferences brings focus and helps us choose careers that will enhance our natural, inherent gifts and talents. Without this knowledge, we remain scattered and unfocused.

This workbook will guide you through this new concept in career decision making and help you focus on your natural strengths. You will be taken on a journey of self-discovery—one that will lead you in making decisions about meaningful work that allows you to express who you truly are.

Sincerely,

Carolyn Kalil

Carolyn Kalil
Counselor

Carolyn Kalil has been inspiring students and organizations for more than 20 years as an educator, counselor, author, speaker and corporate trainer. Her popular book **Follow Your True Colors to the Work You Love** and its companion workbook continue to be successful training tools for students and a number of major corporations, including Warner Brothers and Cisco Systems. And her work is receiving high praise from colleges, prisons, Welfare-to-Work and other programs that strive to help people understand their gifts and talents.

Carolyn earned her Master of Arts degree in counseling from Ohio State University. She resides with her husband in Southern California.

Table of Contents

Chapter 1

Introduction to True Colors

The Meaning Behind the Colors of "True Colors"

Color has long been used as a component of our association and learning process. The physiological impulses generated by certain colors have a marked influence on our lives and can unconsciously mold and guide us in varied directions.

Manufacturers of goods and services recognize the effects of color in regard to marketing products, and industrial designers set the moods of working environments with the use of color. Color can relieve tension and stress and assist in creating tranquil surroundings. It is fitting that the color association concept be adopted in the learning process in lieu of highly technical formulas, symbols, and alphabetical and numerical designations.

Throughout this workbook, you will be constantly fortified with the significance of the four basic colors and their relationship to the subject matter discussed.

Green
Green expresses itself psychologically as the will in operation; as perseverance and tenacity. Green is an expression of firmness and constancy. It indicates constancy of viewpoint as well as constant self-awareness. Green places a high value on the "I" in all forms of possession and self-affirmation.

Persons with green as a primary color want to increase certainty of their own values. They accomplish this either through assertiveness (by holding fast to an idealized perception they have of themselves), or through acknowledgment from others in deference to their possessions—whether greater wealth, or superiority in physical, educational, or cultural attainment.

Blue
Blue represents complete calm. Contemplation of this color effectively pacifies the central nervous system. Blue, like all four basic colors, is a chromatic representation of a basic biological need—in this case, a

physiological tranquillity and a psychological contentment equating to peace and gratification.

Those with blue as a primary color live with balance and harmony and are free of tension; they feel settled, united, and secure.
Blue represents the bands one draws around oneself and others—and a sense of connection. But when allies are involved, blues are especially vulnerable. Consequently, blue corresponds to depth of feeling. Blue, as a relaxed sensitivity, is a prerequisite for empathy, for aesthetic experience, and for meditative awareness.

Orange
Orange represents an energy-expending physiological condition. It is the expression of vital force and of nervous and glandular activity. Thus, it holds the meaning of desire and of all forms of appetite and craving.

Orange is the urge to achieve results and win success; it is hungry to desire all of those things that offer intensity of living and fullness of experience.

Orange is impulse, the will to win, and all forms of vitality and power from sexual potency to revolutionary transformation. It is the impulse toward active doing, toward sport, struggle, competition, eroticism, and enterprising productivity. As impact of the will or the force of will, it corresponds symbolically to the blood of conquest, to the sanguine temperament, and to masculinity. Its sensory perception is appetite; its emotional content is desire; and its organs are the voluntary muscles, the sympathetic nervous system, and the organs of reproduction.

In temporal terms, Orange is the present.

Gold
Gold is sensation as it applies to the bodily senses. It represents a need to be responsible, to fulfill duties and obligations, to organize and to structure lives.

Gold is practical sensibility and punctuality; it is the belief that people should earn their way in life through work and service to others. Gold reflects a need to belong and an effort to carry a share of the load in all areas of living. It is stability, maintained organization, efficiency, and strong concept of home and family—faithful, loyal, and dependable.

How does this color theory impact career planning? If differences make behavior predictable in all contexts, this would also hold true in career decision making. The subsequent chapters will assist each of the color groups in making career decisions that are consistent with who they are.

Theoretical Base

This workbook is based on the belief that we have intrinsic characteristics which drive our human behavior and through which we strive to experience self-esteem. As a result, we are imprinted with specific ways of thinking, understanding, valuing, and conceptualizing.

Our behavior, therefore, manifests certain attitudes, preferences, wants, aims, needs, motives, and desires that make us feel good about ourselves. These predispositions drive our actions and habits, making our behavior predictable in all contexts of our lives.

This theory of individual differences is not new and traces back 25 centuries ago to Hippocrates and, more recently, to Carl Jung who described these differences in his 1921 release of **Psychological Type**.

Soon after, Isabel Myers Briggs developed the now famous Myers Briggs Type Indicator which states that human behavior is quite orderly and can be characterized by 16 different personality types.

Dr. David Keirsey has been refining the work of Myers Briggs for the past 35 years. His book, **Please Understand Me**, reflects the basis of the "True Colors" philosophy.

Don Lowry uses True Colors as a metaphor for understanding human characteristics and how intrinsic behavior must be differentially rewarded. He uses green, blue, orange, and gold—colors that will be used herein to represent each temperament type.

True Colors in comparison to Keirsey's temperament language:

Blue	=	**NF**
Green	=	**NT**
Gold	=	**SJ**
Orange	=	**SP**

A Career Versus a Job

A career is much more than a job. A job is a series of tasks performed for pay, usually without much preparation or concern for personal growth or enjoyment. A career, however, encompasses all of the job characteristics, and more.

One needs to prepare for a career by obtaining required training or education. A career accounts for who a person is, making personality, interests, values, and skills integral parts of a career decision. These considerations allow a career-minded person to continue to grow and to develop, thereby encouraging individual expression and enhanced satisfaction in one's work.

Why Plan a Career?

Generally speaking, most working Americans do not enjoy the work they do. This is because they have chosen a job rather than plan a career that expresses who they are. Since most of us will work 40 hours each week the majority of our lives, the quality of our lives depends greatly on what we do during those precious hours.

The most important component of career planning involves self-understanding. The following chapters will help you understand yourself more thoroughly than ever before. Then you will gather occupational information to assist you in making decisions and setting goals toward a career that can become your life's work.

Chapter 2

Personality Styles

Robert's story

Robert was painfully bored with the third accounting job he'd had in the past four years. Although he began each job with good intentions, he lost interest after the novelty wore off, typically after three or four months on the job. He was convinced that he needed a complete change of direction.

When looking at Robert's personality traits, it was easy to see that he had a tremendous amount of energy, the gift of gab, and a good sense of humor. Yet when asked what he was good at doing, he couldn't think of any particular strengths. He said, "I guess I grew up thinking there wasn't anything good about me. I was the bad apple in the family. You know, the one who caused all the problems. I was always big for my age, and I was known as the class clown who was either telling jokes, throwing spit balls, pulling some girl's hair, or dancing on the table when the teacher left the room. I also had my fair share of fights on the playground. It seemed like I spent as much time in the principal's office as I did in class."

That behavior obviously got him into a lot of trouble, and the only reason why he changed was because a math teacher in high school took special interest in him.

When asked to talk about his positive attributes, he said he was uncomfortable tooting his own horn but "I guess I'm good at persuading and convincing people to do things. I also like to cheer people up and make them laugh. Sometimes I'm accused of saying things inappropriately, like making a funny comment in the middle of a serious and boring business meeting. And unlike some people, who can only do one thing at a time, I like to have several things going on at the same time—maybe this is not such a good thing. I guess I get bored easily and I'm happiest when I'm busy."

These were wonderful examples of Robert's personality traits that he was unaware of as being strengths. When he learned his True Colors he understood that his outgoing, adventurous, free-spirited Orange personality had been suppressed in his accounting job, where he was using his weakest and least rewarding skills.

Robert researched several career options and decided to pursue marketing specialist. He found it especially appealing because it would require him to interact with lots of people on a variety of projects, using print, audio, video, and broadcast media to advertise for clients. To his delight this new career path was a much better match for his particular personality strengths. He explained, "I actually look forward to going to work every day now. I used to think there was something wrong with me because I couldn't sit and concentrate for long periods of time in my accounting job. Now I can see it was the wrong job for me."

Identifying your True Colors will help you discover who you are and the work that is compatible with your personality strengths.

My True Colors

The following exercise will introduce you to True Colors and assist you on a journey of knowing who you are. This knowledge will allow you to be an active participant in life rather than a passenger or a bystander.

Identifying Your True Colors

Step 1: Visualize Yourself

As you read the following passages, look closely at the corresponding color illustrations on the front of each Character Card (included in this book). Do not yet turn over the cards.

Green: "I have this new program for making the organization run like clockwork. Thirty-five years of research, coupled with a computerized network of state-of-the-art equipment will give us a head start on the new program . . ." (New ideas, new technology.)

Blue: "I realize that good material is very necessary to start, but we have to consider the personnel. They have their rights too, you know. After all, Harry's feelings should be considered before starting this program—or anything, for that matter . . ." (Feeling, compassionate, adaptable.)

Orange: "As I see it, the world belongs to those who take action, and 'action' is my middle name! By the time the organizers have it organized, I'll have it done and be ready for something new. So, whattaya say? Let's start now . . ." (Impulsive, immediate, independent.)

Gold: "I think a clear-cut, down-to-business mode will get us to the bottom line here. After all, this institution has been here longer than any of us and it is our responsibility to see that promises are kept and that the program runs smoothly . . ." (Responsible, practical, needs to belong.)

Now that you are familiar with at least a few of the color group characteristics, rank the cards from the one that is most like you to the one that is least like you.

Step 2: Read About Yourself

Turn over the Character Cards and read the back of each. Arrange them again from the one most like you to the one least like you. Rank them in the boxes below using a "4" for the card most like you, down to a "1" for the card least like you.

COURAGEOUS

CONVENTIONAL

COMPASSIONATE

CONCEPTUAL

☐	☐	☐	☐

Step 3: Describe Yourself

Below are several rows of word groups. Working one row at a time, rank each word group in the boxes using a "4" for the group most like you, down to a "1" for the word group least like you. (Score words across.)

Active Opportunistic Spontaneous	☐	Parental Traditional Responsible	☐	Authentic Harmonious Compassionate	☐	Versatile Inventive Competent	☐
Competitive Impetuous Impactful	☐	Practical Sensible Dependable	☐	Unique Empathetic Communicative	☐	Curious Conceptual Knowledgeable	☐
Realistic Open-minded Adventuresome	☐	Loyal Conservative Organized	☐	Devoted Warm Poetic	☐	Theoretical Seeking Ingenious	☐
Daring Impulsive Fun	☐	Concerned Procedural Cooperative	☐	Tender Inspirational Dramatic	☐	Determined Complex Composed	☐
Exciting Courageous Skillful	☐	Orderly Conventional Caring	☐	Vivacious Affectionate Sympathetic	☐	Philosophical Principled Rational	☐

Enter your totals here. (Be sure to include your numbers from Step 2!)

Total Orange	☐	Total Gold	☐	Total Blue	☐	Total Green	☐

Scoring Your True Colors

Now that you have sorted your Character Cards and discovered and read about yourself, have you identified your color spectrum?

Write your color spectrum below. If you are unable to do so at this point, try repeating the process for additional clarity. Or, you may wish to ask people who know you well just how they see you.

My brightest color: ____________________
(The color of your highest total)

My brightest color is shaded with: ____________________
(The color of your second highest total)

And ____________________
(The color of your second lowest total)

With ____________________
(A pale color of your lowest total)

You now know your brightest color, the one which most esteems you. The values of your shaded colors vary in importance and the values of your most pale color are least expressed in your behavior.

Using Your Cards with Others

Keep your Character Cards to use with others. Your friends will have a natural interest in playing True Colors with you. And once you understand their True Colors spectrum, you can utilize the keys to improve communication, as well as your personal, academic, and professional success.

Now, continue reading about your spectrum on the following pages.

The Color Spectrum

Green

Your strength is knowledge! You feel best about yourself when solving problems and when your ideas are recognized, especially when you feel ingenious. You seek to express yourself through your ability to be an expert in everything.

You are a complex individualist with great analytical ability. Your idea of a great day is to use your know-how to create solutions. Although you do not express your emotions openly, you do experience deep feelings.

Your Keys to Personal Success:

Developing models	Abstract thinking
Analytical processes	Exploring ideas
A variety of interests	Striving for competency
Admiring intelligence	Storing wisdom and knowledge
Being a perfectionist	Abhorring redundancy
Utilizing precise language	Handling complexity

You tend to:

Dream of truth, perfection, accuracy
Value answers, resolutions, intelligence, explanations
Regard efficiency, increased output, reduced waste
Dislike injustice and unfairness
Express coolness, calm, and collected reservation
Foster inventions and technology
Respect knowledge and capability
Promote effectiveness, competence, and know-how

Blue

Your strength is authenticity! If your brightest color is blue, you seek to express the inner you. Authenticity and honesty are valued above all other characteristics. You are sensitive to subtlety and—with great flair—you create roles in life's drama. You enjoy close relationships with those you love, and you possess a strong spirituality in your nature.

Making a difference in the world is easy for you because you cultivate the potential in yourself and in others.

Your Keys to Personal Success:

Authenticity as a standard
Devotion to relationships
Assuming creative roles in life's drama
Self-searching
Sensitivity to subtlety
Making a difference in the world
Seeking reality
Cultivating potential of others
Writing and speaking with poetic flair
Having a life of significance
Spirituality
Seeking harmony

You tend to:

Dream of love, affection, and authenticity
Value compassion, sympathy, and rapport
Regard meaning, significance, and identity
Dislike hypocrisy, deception, and insincerity
Express vivacity, enthusiasm, and inspiration
Foster potential growth in people and harmony
Respect nurturing, empathy, and sharing of feelings
Promote growth and development in others

Orange

Your strength is skillfulness! If your brightest color is orange, you need freedom to take immediate action! A zest for life and a desire to test the limits best express your nature. You take pride in being highly skilled in a variety of fields.

You are a master negotiator. Adventure is your middle name. You prefer a hands-on approach to problem solving, and a direct line of reasoning creates the excitement and immediate results that you admire.

Your Keys to Personal Success:

The impulse to really live
The need for variation
Charged adventure
Spontaneous relationships
Being able to act in a crisis
Charm, wit, and fun
Waiting feels like emotional death
Testing the limits
Excitement and lightheartedness
Being a natural entertainer
Taking off for somewhere else
A love of tools
Taking defeats only temporarily

You tend to:

Dream of being free, spontaneity, and impetuousness
Value skills, grace, finesse, and charisma
Regard opportunities, options, and competition
Dislike rigidness, authority, and forcelessness
Express optimism, impatience, eagerness, and confidence
Foster recreation, fun, and enjoyment
Respect skill and artistic expression

Gold

Your strength is duty! If your brightest color is gold, you value order and cherish the traditions of home and family. You provide for and support the structure of society. Steadfastness and loyalty are your trademarks.

Generous and parental by nature, you show you care by making everyone do the right thing. To disregard responsibility of any kind never occurs to you.

Your Keys to Personal Success:

Generosity	The work ethic
A parental nature	Ceremony
A sense of history	Dignity, culture
Perpetuating heritage	Steadfastness
A value of order	Predictability
Home and family	Establishing and organizing institutions

You tend to:

Dream of assets, wealth, influence, status, and security
Value dependability, accountability, and responsibility
Regard service and dedication
Dislike disobedience, non-conformity, and insubordination
Express concern, stability, and purpose
Foster institutions and traditions
Respect loyalty and obligation
Promote groups, ties, bonds, associations, and organizations

My color preferences

Why I think ________________ is my first color

____

____

____

____

____

____

____

____

Why I think ________________ is my second color

____

____

____

____

____

____

____

____

Why I think ________________ is my third color

____

____

____

____

____

____

____

____

Why I think ________________ is my fourth color

____

____

____

____

____

____

____

____

True Colors

Chapter 3

Clarifying Work Values

What's Most Important to Me

Values are the things that matter most to us in our lives and our careers. These things motivate how we think, feel, and behave. When planning a career we need to include our values in our work. As explained in the **Introduction to True Colors**, people value different things. It is important for some people to have a predictable schedule, security, and make lots of money. Others may value having variety, action, and excitement in their work.

Clarifying values is important because a career that is in line with your values will be more enjoyable and provide a sense of meaning in your work.

Anita's Story

Anita was different from everyone else in the family. She loved to perform. Her favorite pastimes were watching TV and going to movies, where she became good at mimicking her favorite characters. In school, she volunteered to be in all the plays and loved hamming it up whenever there was an opportunity to have an audience. Her parents saw this fun loving, creative and artistic side to Anita but discouraged it because they feared she would spend the rest of her life struggling to be successful. To them, acting was not a real job, and they expected her to go to college and study business so that she could find a stable job that paid a lot of money.

When she enrolled in college, she wanted to please her parents, and she also wanted to prove to herself that she could handle classes like accounting, economics and math. But after two years of struggling in these classes, her grades dropped so low that she was dismissed from school. Anita's fragile ego took a devastating blow and her only choice was to look for a job.

After finding work to support herself, Anita enrolled in acting classes at a local community college. These classes truly made her heart sing as she began to recover her self-esteem and a sense of who she was. Through contacts, she landed a better job with a company that trained her to give seminars to motivate people and teach them how to use the company's product. She had fun doing her new work, and her ability to be comfortable in front of an audience made her an exceptional trainer. Although it was not an acting job, the seminar work was enjoyable enough to sustain her. She continued her acting classes at night.

Anita enjoyed school tremendously and she not only earned her bachelor's degree but she continued on to graduate school and received a master's degree in fine arts, specializing in theater. She supported herself by teaching acting classes to college students while she performed at community playhouses at night. Anita felt passionate about inspiring other creative people to pursue their dreams, while she also made a living doing what she loved to do. Her goal was not to become rich and famous, although she thought it would be great to be so fortunate. Her real mission was to use her gifts and talents to serve others through her ability to teach and entertain.

Because Anita's Orange personality thrived on creativity, freedom of expression, spontaneity, fun and excitement, her choice to teach acting and perform served as a perfect outlet for her gifts. These characteristics were her true values, and her peace of mind and success depended on her acknowledging and expressing them.

Prioritizing the following list of values will help you become aware of your true work values.

The True Colors of What's Important to Me (Values and the Four Primary Colors)

In line with personality preferences, those things you value are consistent with your True Colors. Blue values differ from Gold, Green, and Orange values. By acknowledging your preferences, you will better understand your own values.

A. Circle the words that best explain what is important to you.

Authenticity
Being acknowledged
Communication
Compassion
Creativity

Democracy
Emotions
Empathy
Enthusiasm
Friendship
Harmony
Honesty
Individuality
Integrity
Intuition
Love
Natural potential
Optimism
Patience
Peace
Pleasing others
Positive feedback
Public contact
Relationships
Romance
Self-understanding
Sensitivity
Sincerity
Spirituality
Tact
Teamwork
Trustworthiness
Unity

Add the number of words circled above and put the total below.

_______________(total)

B. Circle the words that best explain what is important to you.

Abstraction
Autonomy
Brevity
Cleverness

Competence
Cool-headed under pressure
Creativity
Curiosity
Ethics
Fairness
Focus
Future orientation
Ideas
Imagination
Independence
Ingenuity
Invention
Innovation
Intelligence
Knowledge
Logic
Mental challenge
Objectivity
Precise language
Privacy
Power
Rationality
Self-confidence
Theory
Truth
Vision
Wisdom

Add the number of words circled above and put the total below

________________(total)

C. Circle the words that best explain what is important to you.

Accuracy
Achievement
Affiliation

Authority
Being meticulous
Caution
Community
Compensation
Completion
Conformity
Cooperation
Decisiveness
Dependability
Duty
Efficiency
Facts and data
Family
Justice
Loyalty
Morality
Orderliness
Predictability
Prestige
Profit
Punctuality
Recognition
Religion
Respect
Responsibility
Routine
Rules
Safety
Security
Service
Stability
Status
Structure
Tradition
Wealth

Add the number of words circled above and put the total below.

______________(total)

D. Circle the words that best explain what is important to you.

Action and activity
Adventure
Aesthetics
Artistic creativity
Camaraderie
Change
Competition
Energy
Entertainment
Excitement
Fast pace
Flexibility
Freedom
Fun
Generosity
Humor
Independence
Optimism
Physical challenge
Playfulness
Pleasure
Profit
Skillfulness
Spontaneity
Variety

Add the number of words circled above and put the total below.

_______________(total)

Prioritizing Your Values

List the number of words (values) that you circled in each color group above.

A. ______Blue

C. ______Gold

B. ______Green

D. ______Orange

Which color has the highest number of your values? ____________

Is the order of your total scores consistent with your color spectrum on page 15? Why or why not?

____

____

____

____

____

____

____

____

____

____

Write the five most important values to you from the color that has your highest number of words circled.

1.__________________

2.__________________

3.__________________

4.__________________

5.__________________

True Colors

List two or more careers that you can think of that would require you to have these values. Refer to the Career Pathways for your primary color in Chapter 6 or other resources for more options.

1. ______________________

2. ______________________

3. ______________________

4. ______________________

5. ______________________

Hobbies

A career may not meet all of your values, but the more of them you meet, the more satisfied you will be. Ensure that your additional values are being satisfied through some area of your life; hobbies are a good outlet for expressing values.

List any hobbies you might have.

1.
2.
3.
4.
5.

What values do you recognize through your hobbies?

1.
2.
3.
4.
5.

Chapter 4

Identifying Enjoyable Work Skills

Pre-Test

How well do you know your strengths? You began this workbook with certain beliefs about the things that you do well, and you will continue to learn more about your real strengths. List below all the things you think you are good at.

My strengths are:

1. ______________________________

2. ______________________________

3. ______________________________

4. ______________________________

5. ______________________________

Michelle's Story

Michelle was miserable in a job that she hated. After graduating from high school and majoring in biology in college, she went to work in her parents' restaurant. She had been groomed for the job since she was a child, and when her father's health began to fail, it was her turn to take over. At first Michelle liked the work because it was new and challenging, but she soon began to dread her daily routine.

Michelle described herself as having a very curious mind and being interested in many things. She had always been an avid reader, and she got excellent grades in all her classes in school.

When asked what she disliked most about managing the restaurant, Michelle replied, "I really hate making shift schedules. Invariably someone wants to come in late, leave early or take the day off, which requires me to juggle other people around to maintain adequate coverage. Supervising people is another thing I detest. Some people don't seem to want to work, and to others I have to explain the same thing over and over again before they understand it. I'm not the most patient person and maybe I expect too much from people. It's not that my job is hard work, after all, it's not rocket science. I just feel like I'm going brain dead and wasting my time here."

What Michelle really loved to do was analyze things. "I am constantly picking ideas apart, either with other people or in my own mind. I also love the challenge of problem solving." Her True Colors revealed that some of her other enjoyable skills were diagnosing, interpreting ideas, and researching. She explained that science had always fascinated her. That's why she was attracted to biology as a major. But she got sidetracked from her vision with the restaurant business.

Excited about understanding what she really enjoyed doing, Michelle made a decision to return to school and become a biomedical researcher. She explained, "This career suits me perfectly. It allows me to use my best skills. Maybe someday I will live out my childhood fantasy and become famous for finding a cure for a disease like cancer or AIDS."

Skills

Natural Gifts and Talents and the 4 Primary Colors

To discover your natural gifts and talents—your skills—it is important to identify what you enjoy doing.

We all have an abundance of skills. The question is, which of these skills do we prefer to use in a career? Again, using personality preferences, we can focus on the skills we use naturally and have developed because of preference. An example would be writing with your dominant or preferred hand. You can write with both hands, but you probably write much better with one than the other. When you write with the hand that is preferred, you will do it without struggling and it will flow much better. The same is true when you use your unique gifts and talents. You will experience ease and comfort, and using these skills will seem natural and more enjoyable.

The following lists will help you identify your natural gifts and talents that can be utilized in a variety of occupations. These skills will assist you in understanding what you do best and how they relate to the world of work.

Natural Gifts and Talents

Your natural gifts are things that you are good at and enjoy doing. These skills are not specific to only one type of work. They are called transferable skills because you can take them from one job to another and they can be used in many diverse occupations. They will also give you clues to the work that will give you a sense of meaning and fulfillment.

List #1

Put a check mark next to the skills you most prefer to use.

Acknowledging others—recognizing and validating others for who they are

Building rapport—bringing harmony to a relationship

Building self-esteem—helping others feel good about themselves

Communicating—effectively exchanging verbal or written information with others

Consulting—giving professional advice

Coordinating—bringing people and activities together in a harmonious way

Counseling—helping others with their personal and professional problems

Enlightening—giving spiritual insight

Expressing feelings—openly communicating feelings with other people

Facilitating groups—assisting a group to harmoniously move in a positive direction

Fostering—nurturing

Guiding others—steering or directing people in a positive direction

Healing—restoring health

Helping others—improving the lives of others

Influencing others—having an effect on the lives of other people

Inspiring others—having an exalting influence upon others

Interviewing others—using good communication skills to obtain information from another person

Leading—acting as a positive role model more than being in a position of power or authority

Listening—hearing and paying attention to what others have to say

Mentoring—coaching and supporting others in the direction they want to go

Motivating—acting as a catalyst to move others to action

Nurturing—developing and fostering the potential in others

Public speaking—effectively using language to make speeches in public

Recruiting—getting others involved in whatever they believe in

Supporting others—assisting others emotionally

Teaching—enlightening others and motivating them to learn

Training—directing the growth of others

Visualizing—imagining possibilities

Working as a team—bringing a group together to meet a common goal

Add the total number of check marks above and put your score below.

____

List #2

Put a check mark next to the skills you most prefer to use.

Analyzing—separating or distinguishing the component parts of something to discover its true nature or inner relationships

Conceptualizing—forming abstract ideas in the mind

Consulting—giving technical information or providing ideas to define, clarify or sharpen procedures, capabilities, or product specifications

Critiquing—analyzing, evaluating, or appreciating works of art

Curing—restoring to health after a disease

Debating—discussing a question by considering opposing arguments

Designing—mentally conceiving and planning

Developing—making something available to improve a situation

Diagnosing—analyzing the cause or nature of a condition, situation, or problem

Editing—improving and directing publications

Generating ideas—brainstorming or dreaming up ideas

Intellectualizing—using the intellect rather than emotion or experience

Interpreting ideas—explaining the meaning of ideas

Inventing—developing or creating something for the first time

Learning—gaining knowledge

Observing—examining people, data or things scientifically

Problem solving—identifying key issues or factors in a problem, generating ideas and solutions to solve the problem, selecting the best approach, and testing and evaluating it

Proofreading—reading and marking corrections

Reasoning—thinking

Researching—investigating and experimenting aimed at the discovery and interpretation of facts

Synthesizing—integrating ideas and information

Thinking logically—subjecting ideas to the process of logical thought

Writing—expressing by means of words

Add the total number of check marks above and put the score below.

____

List #3

Put a check mark next to the skills you most prefer to use.

Administering policies—managing a course or method of action

Allocating resources—designating resources for a specific purpose

Attending to detail—paying attention to small items

Bookkeeping—recording the accounts or transactions of a business

Budgeting—planning the amount of money that is available for, required for, or assigned to a particular purpose

Calculating—determining by mathematical means

Caretaking—taking care of the physical needs of others, especially children, the sick and the elderly

Collecting data—gathering information

Coordinating—taking care of logistics for events to flow smoothly

Decision—making—bringing things to a conclusion

Delegating—entrusting responsibilities to other people

Dispatching—sending off or away with promptness

Establishing procedures—constructing a series of steps to be followed in accomplishing something

Estimating cost—judging approximately the value or worth of something

Evaluating—appraising the worth, significance or status of something

Following directions—doing specifically the things you are told to do by others verbally or in writing

Following through—completing an activity planned or begun

Guarding—protecting or defending

Maintaining schedules—overseeing something designated for a fixed, future time

Maintaining records—accurate and up-to-date record-keeping

Managing—directing or conducting business or affairs

Monitoring—watching, observing, or checking for a specific purpose

Organizing—arranging things in a systematic order

Paying attention to detail—looking for smaller elements

Planning—making a way of proceeding

Preparing—getting something ready for use or getting ready for some occasion

Recording—putting things in writing

Regulating—governing or directing according to rule or law

Securing—relieving from exposure to danger

Serving—making a contribution to the welfare of others

Supervising—taking responsibility for the work done by others

Add the total number of check marks above and put the score below.

____

List #4

Put a check mark next to the skills you most prefer to use.

Assembling things—fitting together the parts of things

Coaching—training intensively by instruction, demonstration, and practice

Competing—challenging another for the purpose of winning

Constructing—building something

Dancing—performing rhythmic and patterned bodily movements, usually to music

Displaying things—arranging something in an eye-catching exhibit

Drafting—drawing the preliminary sketch, version, or plan for something

Entertaining—performing publicly for amusement

Gardening—cultivating a plot of ground with herbs, fruits, flowers or vegetables

Illustrating—providing visual features intended to explain or decorate

Influencing others—causing an effect on others

Manipulating—treating or operating with the hands or by mechanical means

Manufacturing—making from raw materials by hand or by machinery

Marketing—planning and strategizing how to present a product or service in the marketplace

Negotiating—conferring with another so as to arrive at the settlement of some matter

Operating tools—skillfully handling tools to perform work

Operating vehicles—driving cabs, limousines, heavy equipment, etc.

Performing—practicing an art that involves public performance

Persuading—influencing others in favor of a product, service, or point of view

Promoting—persuading people to see the value of an idea, person, activity, or cause

Public speaking—expressing yourself before a group

Repairing—restoring by replacing a part or putting together what is torn or broken

Responding to emergencies—being spontaneous and level-headed in emergency situations

Risk taking—having a dangerous element to life

Selling—promoting a service or product with the intent of getting someone to buy or accept it in exchange for something, usually money

Add the total number of check marks and put the score below.

____

Write in the total scores from each list above and circle your highest score.

List #1 ___________

List #2 ___________

List #3 ___________

List #4 ___________

Find the description of your highest score below. (Chapter 6 will discuss in more detail.)

#1. Your natural gifts and talents are: **Blue** (Notice how many of your skills involve helping other people improve their lives.)

#2. Your natural gifts and talents are: **Green** (Notice how many of your skills involve mental activity and problem solving.)

#3. Your natural gifts and talents are: **Gold** (Notice how many of your skills involve attending to details, implementation, and follow-through.)

#4. Your natural gifts and talents are: **Orange** (Notice how many of your skills involve actively doing a variety of things.)

List your favorite skills from your color group.

1. ___________________
2. ___________________
3. ___________________
4. ___________________
5. ___________________

True Colors

List two or more careers that require you to have these skills or natural gifts and talents. Refer to the Career Pathways in Chapter 6 or other resources for more options.

1. ____________________

2. ____________________

3. ____________________

4. ____________________

5. ____________________

Post-test

My first color represents my major strengths, the things I do well.
My strengths are:

1. ____________________

2. ____________________

3. ____________________

4. ____________________

5. ____________________

6. ____________________

7. ____________________

8. ____________________

9. ____________________

10. ____________________

True Colors

My last color represents my weaknesses, the things I do not do as well. My weaknesses are:

1. ______________________________
2. ______________________________
3. ______________________________
4. ______________________________
5. ______________________________
6. ______________________________
7. ______________________________
8. ______________________________
9. ______________________________
10. ______________________________

Capitalize on your strengths; they are most important to use in your work. Know what you are good at and focus on those areas. Also, understand your weaknesses in order to manage them. Improve these areas as needed, but with less emphasis on them in the workplace.

True Colors

Summarize what you have learned about yourself in this chapter.

____

____

____

____

____

Chapter 5

The True Colors of My Self-Esteem

One-minute exercise

Write one positive thing about yourself on each line.

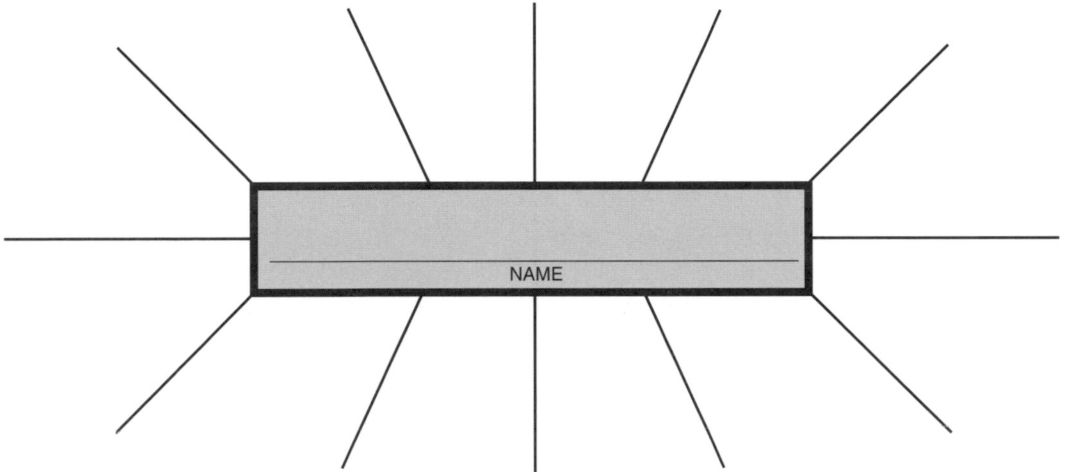

Was this exercise easy or difficult? Why?

The more positive thoughts you have about yourself, the higher your self-esteem will be.

Self-esteem is an inside job. It is intrinsic and as natural as breathing. You do not need to do anything other than be who you are to feel good about yourself. You already have what it takes to experience self-esteem, and it belongs to you as your human right.

We have been led to believe that if we have all the material success we desire, we will feel good about ourselves. In reality, the opposite is true. We only need to be who we are and do what we love in order to have what we desire. If we feel good about ourselves we can have all of those other things. That is why it is so difficult for some people to achieve success—they are doing things in the reverse.

Our self-perceptions drive us in a direction toward success or in a direction away from it. Our natural strengths are our built-in program for self-esteem and success, and it is with these unique gifts and talents that we will begin our examination of career decision making.

This chapter, as well as subsequent ones, will give you the knowledge you require to begin the road to high self-esteem and success.

Self-Esteeming Characteristics by Color Group

Let's take a look at the self-esteem characteristics manifest in the four primary color groups.

Green: The Need to be Ingenious

As a Green, you are in esteem when you feel competent. You want to understand and control the realities of life. This control represents the power to acquire the multiple abilities for which you pride yourself.

You feel best about yourself when you are solving problems and when your ideas are recognized. You are a complex individualist with great analytical ability. Although you do not express you emotions openly, you do experience deep feelings.

An abstract thinker, you are symbolized by the vision of the genius; the challenge of science; the complexity of models and systems; and in the perfection of symmetry, such as that demonstrated in the great pyramids.

You thrive on your mental competencies as well as on the skills and abilities of others. And you are motivated by a quest for knowledge and the ability to seek it and provide it. The control of knowledge is as important as its acquisition because such control can be perceived as power.

More about Greens:

Motivated to improve—The performance aspect of knowledge is not of primary concern. You prefer, rather, to provide information for others to act upon. From those results, you are motivated even further to improve on that which you have previously perceived or created. The importance and emphasis on performance concerns you only when it is your own, as with the development of an idea or the pursuit of new knowledge.

Language as a communication tool—The Green personality seeks gratification in professions which rely on competence, including the sciences, engineering, computers and mathematics, philosophy, and any field which requires precise detailing of ideas. Language and its use are merely toys with which to play; you have a certain fascination with language as a communication tool.

Relationships on an intellectual level—Relationships you establish with others may appear to be only on an intellectual level. This tends to cause others to be unfeeling and distant. Your enthusiasm in directing attention only to those with whom you share a mental rapport is seen as withholding thoughts and emotions from others.

Working as a source of pleasure—As a Green, you derive genuine pleasure from work because it represents a continual quest for knowledge. Work is the means of providing creature comforts and also a source of recreation. On any day away from your regular work, you are content to sit before the television and listen only to informational programs. To be mentally idle is to be worthless.

Detaching to determine the "why"—Because you often detach or step back to reflect the "why" of your experiences, that detachment may prevent you from having the experience yourself. You may feel that the experience itself may not be required to comprehend it.

Blue: The Need to be Authentic

As a Blue, you are in esteem when you are authentic. You must find your real self and live your life as an expression of your unique identity. Integrity means unity of inner self with outer expression.

Life is a dream in which you must find meaning. You are sensitive to subtlety and create roles—with special flair—in life's drama. You enjoy close relationships with those you love and experience a spiritual pride in your nature. Making a difference in the world comes easily as you cultivate the potential in yourself and in others.

A natural harmonizer, you are symbolized by the vision of peace; the romance of love ballads; the drama of stage and screen; the importance of people; and the warmth of a hug and a handshake.

The exclusive Blue segment maintains a powerful influence over the rest of society, in that so many creative writers belong to this color grouping. Journalists, poets, playwrights, novelists, and biographers who are generally motivated to inspire others are nearly exclusively of the Blue personality type.

More about Blues:

Continuing the search for self—From childhood, the enigmatic and continual search for self began, and it continues to this day. Human relationships are of primary concern to you, not only on a one-on-one basis, but among the people of the world, as well. You often behave with almost chameleon ability to preserve a personal relationship. You even will be that which others want you to be in order to provide an atmosphere of harmony. You explore and consume new directions, ideas, and conceptions dealing with human relationships. You romanticize your own experiences and those of others in an effort to bring importance to the energy expended.

Relating on a personal level—You relate best to others on a personal level. This leads you into professions such as psychology, counseling, teaching, social work, and the ministry. Communication is such a part of your life that in these professions you are able to express your concerns with poetic license and with flair. You treat your work almost in a missionary sense, with the emphasis on those benefits that will be derived rather than on the job itself. You devote more time than any other color group to developing this personal aspect because you seek the same fulfillment for yourself that you attempt to give to others.

Seeking identity through contribution—You seek identity through contribution. The significance of the contribution need not bring personal acknowledgment, and in many cases you receive fewer rewards than do all other color groups. But you continue to pursue those esoteric goals which you feel are neglected by society.

Seeing things through to the end—Time is not captive to you. When involved in a meaningful personal relationship or working on a project which requires an inordinate amount of time, you have a compulsion to see it through to the end. You consider the time well spent, not only as a benefit to yourself, but because you feel that if you could not provide the attention, it would probably not be provided by others.

Tapping into universal harmony—You enjoy a natural affinity with nature and with all phenomena of the human experience. You attempt to tap into what you perceive to be the harmony of the universe in all that you do and experience.

Orange: The Need to be Skillful

As an Orange, you are in esteem when, above all, you are free to act on a moment's notice. You choose to be impulsive and act upon the idea of the moment. Action or doing carries its own reward.

Adventure is your middle name, and you do things for the joy of doing. A zest for life and a desire to test the limits exemplify your Orange personality. You take pride in being highly skilled in a variety of fields, and are a master negotiator. Your hands-on approach to problem solving and direct line of reasoning creates excitement and immediate results.

Your free spirit is symbolized by the flight of an eagle; the sensation of hang-gliding; the action and risk of driving a motorcycle; the skillfulness of handling a tool; and the freedom of the out-of-doors.

Your Orange personality's zest for action and freedom are as much a part of the culture of this country as are the tradition and duty of the Gold personality.

More about Oranges:

Acting on impulse—You thrive on being able to act on impulse—to be expressive without reluctance. Professions which intrigue and excite you include the world of entertainment, athletics, and those art forms which demand skill, such as photography, dance, and music. Orange personality types are also attracted to law enforcement. It is the passion which accompanies skill that provides lure for the Orange.

Enjoying new ideas and goals—Life to the Orange is a series of new situations, new ideas, and new goals. Rules are recognized, but broken if necessary. You enjoy owning tools, gadgets, or anything representing newer, faster, and better methods to accomplish a goal. Keeping things on an even keel is not your strong suit. Change, to you, is not only exciting, but often preferable.

Being with people—You enjoy being with people and are often the recognized leader. You easily run interference for others, relishing an opportunity to reflect the importance of doing so. You generate a genuine camaraderie with others using your gregarious nature to evoke trust from them.

Dealing with pressure—You deal with pressure and physical demands far more easily than do other color groups. The adage, "no pain, no gain," is a byword for you. That kind of stamina provides the backdrop for your competitive nature, a nature from which you derive pleasure. This competitiveness also means that you will achieve goals with perfection.

Being misunderstood—Orange types are at times perceived to be less than sensitive to others. You are often misunderstood in your drive to accomplish something with only the end result in mind. While others may be charmed by your ability and enthusiasm, they can also become confused by your unorthodox methods.

Acting without reservation—Freedom is your ultimate pleasure—freedom to act without reservation, to make decisions without approval or obligation. You enjoy boundless energy which you believe should be used to its highest potential. Life is an adventure and you believe you know exactly how to make the best of it.

Gold: The Need to be Responsible

As a Gold, you are in esteem when you feel responsible and belong to a social unit. Regardless of which social unit is involved, you feel you must earn your place of belonging by being useful, fulfilling responsibilities, being of service, and caring for others.

Steadfastness and loyalty are your trademarks; you value order and cherish traditions of home and family. You are generous and parental, demonstrating that you care by ensuring that everyone does the right thing.

The backbones of society, Golds are symbolized in the patriotism of the American flag; the structure of groups and organizations; the security of banks and savings books; the responsibility of parenting; the caring of nursing and healing; and the pride of lineage and aristocracy.

From the moment your personality began to develop, a sense of obligation and duty also began to emerge. Rules by which people interact are of utmost concern to you. Security of the family unit and for all it stands is the foundation by which all other interactions are expressed, be it in the school, the workplace, the church, social units, or society itself.

More about Golds:

Finding comfort in structure—Examples of the Gold structure are edified early in life. Organizations such as the Boy Scouts and Girl Scouts are the groundwork for the future comfort zones of Golds. You are drawn to service organizations, making the time spent in these activities almost your recreation. To be part of an organization makes you feel as if you are the organization; titles, banners, flags, and similar forms of identification are necessary symbols representing the physical stamps of approval for your behavior.

Enjoying responsibility —For you, responsibility is a blessing. You are the premier conservator on continuity and perpetuity. Even the apparent "dumping" on you of those duties others will not perform cannot dissuade you from your continuing quest for responsibility.

Providing standards to society—You have a distinct concern for others, which differs from that of a Blue personality. Your concern is to provide standards within the society to better enable people to tend to obligations. The financial world is the domain of the Gold. Education, medicine, and service occupations are all areas to which you are drawn.

Revering history—You have a reverence for history and its importance, and from this you develop a background for stability and the perpetuity of institutions. Change represents a threat to you. Social change must come slowly and methodically, and in the workplace changes must come only after research and cooperation. You do not support revolutionary changes or those that appear to be merely "Band-Aids" or quick fixes.

Establishing stability—Your sense of duty comes from having established stability and strength in your life pattern. You express yourself with concrete examples of your Gold personality, be it with your family, home, job, or social activities. These represent your basic motivation and direction, and society esteems you because you exemplify that which society itself strives to accomplish.

What Makes Me Feel Good?

As a _______________ person, I have learned that what makes me feel good

about myself is ____

____

____

____

____

Name two careers that you can think of that would make you feel **good** about yourself.

1. ______________________________

2. ______________________________

What to Look for When You're Out of Esteem

There are certain symptoms you can look for when having a bad day—when you are either out or running out of esteem. You can learn to recognize these characteristics, which are generally related to your particular color grouping.

Green
Indecisiveness
Refusal to comply or cooperate
Extreme aloofness and withdrawal
Snobbish, put-down remarks, and sarcasm
Refusal to communicate; the silent treatment
Perfectionism due to severe performance anxiety
Highly critical attitudes toward yourself or others

True Colors

Blue
Attention-getting misbehavior
Lying to save face
Withdrawal
Fantasy, day-dreaming, and trancing out
Crying and depression
Passive resistance
Yelling and screaming

Orange
Rudeness and defiance
Breaking the rules intentionally
Running away and dropping out
Use of stimulants
Acting out boisterously
Lying and cheating
Physical aggressiveness

Gold
Complaining and self-pity
Anxiety and worry
Depression and fatigue
Psychosomatic problems
Malicious judgments about yourself or others
Herd mentality exhibited in blind following of leaders
Authoritarianism and phobic reactions

Out-of-Esteem Behavior

Describe a time when you felt out-of-esteem.

____

____

____

____

How to regain Self-Esteem

What did you do or could have done to regain your self-esteem? Review your self-esteeming characteristics for ideas.

True Colors

Self-Talk

What are you saying to yourself? Self-talk includes all the thoughts and messages we say to ourselves. It is well documented that what you say about and to yourself affects your mental, emotional and physical well-being. Much of this silent, mindless chatter is negative and very destructive. Try to catch yourself when you say things like, "I can't pass this class no matter what I do," or, "I'm not as smart as _______."

Positive Self-Talk

You can change negative self-talk by reprogramming your mind. It is a matter of training your mind to say positive things to yourself. First you must be aware and listen to how you talk to yourself. Begin to become conscious of this behavior by recording what you say. The use of affirmations is an effective tool to change this inner dialog into positive statements about yourself. An affirmation would be to say, "I can pass this class."

Negative Self-Talk

List some of the negative statements you have made to yourself. Example: "I'm not smart enough."

1. ______________________________

2. ______________________________

3. ______________________________

4. ______________________________

5. ______________________________

6. ______________________________

7. ______________________________

8. ______________________________

9. ______________________________

10. ______________________________

Change each of the negative statements into a positive one (affirmation). Example: "I am smart."

1. ______________________________

2. ______________________________

3. ______________________________

4. ______________________________

5. ______________________________

6. ______________________________

7. ______________________________

8. ______________________________

9. ______________________________

10. ______________________________

Chapter 6

Career Pathways by Color Groupings

Now that you are familiar with your True Colors, this chapter will assist you in selecting a career pathway that fits your personality, needs, and strengths. It will provide you with an area of focus and a variety of occupational choices from entry level careers to professional ones that require specialized training, a college education and /or experience.

The average person will change their career 4-7 times in their lifetime. The four career pathways below will be listed with each color group providing several suitable options to choose from. The occupations within the same cluster will be helpful to return to when considering future career possibilities.

4 Career Pathways

- Arts and Communications
- Engineering, Industrial and Scientific Technology
- Health, Human and Consumer Services
- Business/Office

Scan the following pages to find the careers list that corresponds with your first color.

Orange Careers

Orange men and women are action oriented. They are highly resourceful and sell a product, an idea, or a project in a way no other color can. However, their lack of interest in administrative details and follow-through makes them the target of blame and criticism within an organization. When striking out on their own, they must have someone to follow-through if they are to be successful. When the Orange need for excitement and promotional talents are used to constructive ends, any institution is fortunate to have them as employees. However, if these energies are not channeled correctly, destructive and anti-social activities will result. Confining rules and regulations and day-to-day routines are deadly to Orange. Above all else, they seek excitement in their work.

Some examples of careers that you may find interesting are listed below. Remember, you are not limited to these options; refer to the recommended resources in Chapter 8 to generate additional options.

Exercise

Circle the careers that are of interest to you.

Arts and Communications

Entry level careers (Require on-the-job training and/or minimal experience):

Broadcast Technician
Dancer
Design Assistant
Disc Jockey
Floral Shop Clerk
Instrumentalist
Layout/Paste-Up Artist
Lighting Technician
Merchandise Displayer
Model
Motion Picture Projectionist
Movie/TV Extra
Music Copier
Photographer's Assistant
Photojournalist
Singer
Sound Technician
Stagehand
Window Display Person

Careers that require training, a college education, and/or experience:

Acting Coach
Actor/Actress
Advertising
Announcer
Art Teacher
Camera Operator
Cartoonist
Ceramist
Choral Director
Choreographer
Comedian

Cruise Director
Dance Studio Manager
Dancer
Drama Teacher
Fabric Artist
Fashion Designer
Fashion Designer
Film Dubber
Floral Designer
Illustrator
Instrument Repairer
Interior Designer
Landscape Architect
Massage Therapist
Music Teacher
Photographer
Piano Tuner
Print Maker
Printer
Private Music Teacher
Public Relations Specialist
Recording Studio Assistant
Sculptor
Singer
Sound Engineer
Textile Designer
Theater Arts Technician
Theater Manager

Engineering, Industrial and Scientific Technology

Entry level careers (Require on-the-job training and/or minimal experience):

Apprentice Carpenter
Auto-Body
Bicycle Repairperson
Cabinet Maker's Assistant
Electronic Assembler
Iron Worker

Jeweler Assistant
Junior Drafter
Machine Shop Assistant
Mechanics Assistant
Metal Fabricator
Painter Assistant/car
Painter/car
Service Station Attendant
Welder's Helper
Welder-Cutter

Careers that require training, community college, and/or experience:

Air Conditioner Mechanic
Automotive Electrician
Automotive Technician
Aviation Maintenance Technician
Cabinet Maker
Carpenter
Computer Electronics Technician
Computer Repairer
Construction Technology
Dental Lab Technician
Drafter
Electrical Engineer
Electrician
Electronics Technician
Engineering Technician
Equipment Operator
Heavy Duty Mechanic
Heavy Equipment Operator
Instrumentation Technician
Iron Worker
Jeweler
Machinist
Mason
Mechanical Engineer
Mechanical Engineering Technician
Office Machine Technician

Ophthalmic Lab Technician
Parts Manager
Plumber
Robotics Mechanic
Shop Owner
Surveyor
Tool and Die Maker
Trade and Industrial Teacher
Welder/Cutter
Welder/Fitter
Wood Technology Instructor

Health, Human and Consumer Services

Entry level careers (Require on-the-job training and/or minimal experience):

Baking Assistant
Bartender
Cake Decorator
Caterer
Child Care Aide
Classroom Aide
Cook
Fire Cadet
Fitness/Aerobics Instructor
Food Processing
Home Equipment Sales
Home Health Assistant
Lifeguard
Maintenance Grounds/Buildings
Nanny
Nursing Home Aide
Playground Supervisor
Police Cadet
Pre-School Child Care
Receptionist
Recreation Assistant/Aide
Restaurant hostess
Self-Employed (Crafts)

Teacher's Aide
Waiter/Waitress
Youth Toy/Clothing Consultant

Careers that require training, a college education, and/or experience:

Adult Education/Vocational Teacher
Adult, Youth Recreation Program Director
Assistant Clothing Buyer
Athletic Trainer
Beautician/Barber
Chef/Baker
Child Development Specialist
Children's Wear Designer
Chiropractor
Display Designer
Early Childhood Educator
Emergency Room Medical Doctor
Emergency Room Nurse
Executive Chef
Fashion Buyer
Fashion Display Person
Fashion Journalist/Photographer
Firefighter
Flight Attendant
Floral Designer
Furniture Builder/Restorer
Game Official
Interior Designer
Juvenile Court Probation Worker
Paramedic/EMT
Party Planner
Pediatrician
Photographer
Physical Education Teacher/Coach
Physical Therapist
Police Officer
Politician
Pre-School Teacher
Professional Athlete

Public Speaker
Recreational Therapist
Sales/Catering Manager
Speech Teacher
Sports Announcer
Sports Medicine
Tailor
Telecommunications
Travel Agent
Trial Lawyer
Wildland Fire Suppressor

Business/Office Careers

Entry level careers (Require on-the-job training and/or minimal experience):

Computer operator
Independent Small Business Owner
Real Estate Sales
Salesperson
Telephone Solicitor

Careers that require training, a college education, and/or experience:

Advertising
Buyer
Computer Programmer
Corporate Lawyer
Fashion Merchandiser
Marketing
Sales Agent

Which career pathway has the highest number of careers circled?

____

You may want to research other resources for more options in this particular pathway.

Gold Careers

Gold persons are realistic, matter-of-fact, and more curious about new products than they are about new ideas and theories. They are very good at following procedures, rules, and regulations. They prefer work environments in which duties and authorities are well defined, and where they can be rewarded through hard work and feel valued as responsible and dependable employees. Their interest in thoroughness, pragmatism, punctuality, and efficiency leads them to occupations in which these preferences are appreciated.

Some examples of careers that you may find interesting are listed below. Remember, you are not limited to these options; refer to the recommended resources in Chapter 8 to generate additional options.

Exercise

Circle the careers that are of interest to you.

Business/Office Careers

Entry level careers (Require on-the-job training and/or minimal experience):

Bank Teller
Bookkeeper
Cashier
Clerk Typist
Computer Operator
Data Entry Clerk
Department Supervisor
Dispatcher
File Clerk
Insurance Clerk
Loan Officer
Payroll Clerk
Receptionist
Retail Clerk
Stock Clerk
Telephone Operator
Ticket Agent
Transcriptionist
Travel Reservations Agent

Careers that require training, a college education, and/or experience:

Accounting Clerk
Accounting/CPA
Administrative Assistant
Auditing Clerk
Auditor
Bank Examiner
Claims Agent
Computer Operator
Court Reporter
Executive Secretary
Financial Planner
Hospital Administrator
Human Resources Manager
Insurance Sales
Legal Transcriber
Manager Financial Institution
Medical Records Clerk
Medical Transcriptionist
Office Manager
Paralegal Secretary
Programmer
Property Manager
Public Health Administration
Purchasing Agent
Stenographer
Work Processor

Health, Human and Consumer Services

Entry level careers (Require on-the-job training and/or minimal experience):

Banking Assistant
Child Care Aide
Closet Organizer
Dry Cleaners/Alterations
File Clerk
Garment Fitter

Geriatrics Aide
Home Health Aide
Home Health Assistant
Hospital Aide
Library Clerk
Military Service
Nanny
Nursing Home Aide
Orderly
Police Cadet
Postal Employee
Restaurant Cook
Secretaries
Security Officer
Sewing Machine Operator
Social Welfare Trainee
Teacher's Aide
Tutor
Upholsterer

Careers that require training, a college education, and/or experience:

Child Development Institutional Manager
Child Development Specialist
Child Development Teacher
Clinical Lab Technician
Conference Manager
Corrections Officer
Court Reporter
Dental Assistant
Dental Hygienist
Dentist
Department Store Manager
Dry Cleaner Owner
Elementary School Teacher
Executive Secretary
Food Magazine Editor
Food Service Manager
Group Home Supervisor
Home Economics Teacher

Hotel/Motel Manager
In-Home Health Care Provider
Judge
Lawyer
Legal Secretary
Librarian
Library Technician
Licensed Vocational Nurse
Medical Doctor
Medical Records Clerk
Medical Records Technician
Medical Transcriptionist
Military Officer
Nutritionist
Paralegal Assistant
Pharmacist
Police Officer
Public Administrator
Public Housing Consultant
Registered Dietician
Registered Nurse
Respiratory Therapist
Restaurant Manager
School Administrative Assistant
School Administrator
School Counselor
Secondary School Teacher
Security Service Person
Social Worker
X-ray Technician

Engineering, Industrial and Scientific Technology

Entry level careers (Require on-the-job training and/or minimal experience):

Animal Caretaker
Fish Hatchery Worker
Flower Grower
Forester Aide

Harvester
Irrigator
Range Manager/Worker
Sheep Shearer
Tree Pruner

Careers that require training, a college education, and/or experience:

Agriculture Engineer
Crop Duster
Farm Supervisor
Farmer
Fish and Game Warden
Fishery Resource Manager
Industrial Engineer
Logging Operations Inspector
Mineral/Mining Engineer
Orchard Supervisor
Park Ranger
Pest Inspector
Sanitary Engineer
Soil engineer
Soil Technologist
Structural Engineer
Timber Manager
Wildlife Manager
Wildlife Technician

Which career pathway has the highest number of careers circled?

____

You may want to research other resources for more options in this particular pathway.

Blue Careers

Blue persons have remarkable latitude in career choices and they succeed in many fields. They are imaginative, enthusiastic, and can do almost anything that is of interest to them. At work, they are at ease with colleagues, and others enjoy their presence. They are highly creative in dealing with people and are outstanding at inspiring group spirit and getting people together. Blues are likely to lose interest in their job once people or projects become routine. They prefer a family-like, friendly, personalized, and warm work environment. They dislike jobs that require painstaking detail and follow-through over a period of time. They prefer people-oriented careers and job opportunities that allow creativity and variety in day-to-day operations.

Some examples of careers that you may find interesting are listed below. Remember, you are not limited to these options; refer to the recommended resources in Chapter 8 for additional options.

Exercise

Circle the careers that are of interest to you.

Health, Human and Consumer Services

Entry level careers (Require on-the-job training and/or minimal experience):

Aerobics Teacher
Child Care Aide
Department Store Clerk (Clothing)
Fund-Raiser
Home Health Assistant
Hospital Interpreter
Host/Hostess
Pre-School Child Care
Receptionist
Skin Care Specialist
Social Welfare Trainee
Tour Guide
Tutor
Wardrobe Consultant
Wedding Consultant
Weight Loss Counselor

Careers that require training, a college education, and/or experience:

Adult Education -Vocational Teacher
Airline Receptionist
Art Therapist
Career Center Technician
Career Coach
Career Counselor
Child Development Specialist
Child Development Teacher
Child Psychologist
College Professor
Community Affairs Coordinator
Drug and Alcohol Counselor
Education Consultant
Elementary School Teacher
Employment Interviewer
English Teacher
Family Lawyer
Fashion Journalist
Fashion Writer
Fashion/Fabric Designer
Flight Attendant
Foreign Language Teacher
Group Home Supervisor
Gynecologist
Human Service Worker
Hypnotherapist
Lawyer for Battered Women
Marriage and Family Therapist
Medical Social Worker
Minister
Motivational Speaker
Nun
Nutritional Consultant
Pediatrician
Personal Coach
Pre-School Teacher
Psychiatric Social Worker
Psychology Teacher

Public Housing Consultant
Public Relations Specialist
Rehabilitation Counselor
School Counselor
Social Services Specialist
Social Worker
Speech Coach
Spiritual Counselor
Team Building Consultant
Training Specialist
Wedding Consultant

Arts and Communication

Entry level careers (Require on-the-job training and/or minimal experience):

Dancer
Model
Singer

Careers that require training, a college education, and/or experience:

Actor
Art Teacher
Children's Book Illustrator
Children's Book Writer
Drama Teacher
Fashion Designer
Foreign Language Interpreter/Translator
Greeting Card Writer
Interior Designer
Jingle Writer
Journalism Professor
Journalist
Music Teacher
Non-fiction Writer
Poet
Public Relations

Romance Novelist
Talk Show Host

Which career pathway has the highest number of careers circled?

___

You may want to research other resources for more options in this particular pathway.

Green Careers

Greens are the most reluctant of all the colors to do things in a traditional manner. They are always on the lookout for new projects, new activities, and new procedures. This accounts for their tendency to become entrepreneurs and to work for themselves. Greens can succeed in a variety of occupations as long as the job does not involve too much humdrum routine. They tend to lose interest once their work is no longer challenging, and they may fail to follow thorough, often to the discomfort of colleagues. As an employee, the Green person might work against the system just for the joy of being one-up. However, this type can contribute immensely in a work atmosphere that allows independence and expression of ingenuity.

Some examples of careers that you may find interesting are listed below. Remember, you are not limited to these options; refer to the recommended resources in Chapter 8 to generate additional options.

Exercise

Circle the careers that are of interest to you.

Engineering, Industrial and Scientific Technology

Careers that require training, a college education, and/or experience:

Aeronautical Engineer
Aerospace Engineer
Agriculture Engineer
Animal Breeder

Animal Science Technician
Architect
Automotive Engineer
Automotive Instructor
Automotive Research and Development
Biomedical Engineer
Chemical Engineer
Civil Engineer
Computer Engineer
Conservationist
Entomologist
Environmental Designer
Environmental Engineer
Environmental Scientist
Marine Biologist
Marine Engineer
Meteorological Analyst
Organic Chemist
Plant Geneticist
Seed Analyst

Arts and Communications

Careers that require training, a college education, and/or experience:

Actor/Actress
Advertising
Architect
Art Advisor
Art Restorer
Camera Operator
Classified Ad Writer
Columnist
Conductor
Copy Writer
Critic
Editor
Freelance Writer
Ghost Writer

Graphic Artist
Journalist
Literary Agent
Literary Writer
Lyricist
Music Composer
Music Teacher
News Writer
Photographer
Playwright
Producer
Publisher
Science Fiction Writer
Screen Writer
Sound Engineer
Speech Writer
Television Script Writer
Textbook Writer

Health, Human and Consumer Services

Careers that require training, a college education, and/or experience:

Acupuncturist
Anthropologist
Biomedical Researcher
College Professor/Researcher
Consumer Advocate
Doctor Internal Medicine
Fashion/Fabric Designer
FBI Agent
Home Energy Consultant
Lawyer
Math Teacher
Medical Assistant
Nuclear Medicine Technology
Physician's Assistant
Podiatrist
Police Detective
Psychiatrist

Psychologist
Speech Pathologist
Speech Therapist
Surgeon
Surgical Technician
Veterinarian

Business/Office Careers

Careers that require training, a college education, and/or experience:

Advertising
Chief Executive Officer (CEO)
Computer Network Engineer
Computer Programmer
Independent Small Business Owner
Marketing

Which career pathway has the highest number of careers circled?

____

You may want to research other resources for more options in this particular pathway.

Exercise

List the top five careers that you are most interested in learning more about. You may want to include those listed in Chapters 3, 4, and 5.

1.____________________________

2.____________________________

3.____________________________

4.____________________________

5.____________________________

Chapter 7

Smart Comes in 4 Colors

Personal Motivation Determines Learning Styles

The purpose of this chapter is to discuss what motivates you to learn and discover your ideal learning environment. Because we don't all learn the same way, it is important to know your best style. This information will help you understand what you need to thrive in the classroom. You will also learn which teachers are compatible with your particular learning style.

ORANGE

Learning Motivators for Orange Students

- Perform well in competition, especially when there is a lot of action
- Love games and "hands-on" activities
- Love fun and excitement
- Have difficulty with routine or structured presentations
- Receive a kick out of putting what they have learned to immediate use
- Perform best when they can apply skills learned in school to the world in which they live
- Learn by doing

Atmosphere in which Orange Students Learn Best

- Spontaneous
- Animated, active
- Humorous
- Interactive
- Minimal lectures
- Friendly

Positive learning experience

Give an example of a positive learning experience that you have had.

What is the relationship between this experience and what motivates you to learn?

GOLD

Learning Motivators for Gold Students
- Do their best when the course content is structured and clearly defined
- Want to know when they are on the right track
- Are greatly helped by rules and directions
- Thrive on routine and orderliness

Atmosphere in which Gold Students Learn Best
- Structured
- Tasks clearly stated
- Organized
- Clear expectations

Positive learning experience
Give an example of a positive learning experience that you have had.

What is the relationship between this experience and what motivates you to learn?

GREEN

Learning Motivators for Green Students

- Perform best when exposed to the driving force or overall theory behind a subject
- Prefer to work independently
- Aroused by new ideas and concepts, and enjoy interpreting them before adding them to their bank of knowledge
- Need to be challenged
- Like to be recognized and appreciated for their competence in a subject

Atmosphere in which Green Students Learn Best

- Academically demanding
- Encouragement to learn more
- Energetic programs

Positive learning experience

Give an example of a positive learning experience that you have had.

What is the relationship between this experience and what motivates you to learn?

BLUE

Learning Motivators for Blue Students

- Feel best in an open, interactive atmosphere
- Like to feel that their teachers really care about them, and that they give the class a personal touch
- Appreciate supportive attention and feedback
- Thrive in a "humanistic," people-oriented environment
- "Turn off" when conflicts arise, and flourish in an atmosphere of cooperation
- Important that teachers value and respect their feelings

Atmosphere in which Blue Students Learn Best

- Warm
- Relaxed
- Creative
- Flexible
- Caring, happy
- Discussion-oriented
- Freedom to experiment
- Personal

Positive learning experience

Give an example of a positive learning experience that you have had.

What is the relationship between this experience and what motivates you to learn?

____

____

____

____

Teaching Styles

Teaching styles differ depending on the teacher's color or personality. Since personal values dictate what motivates a person's behavior, they will indicate what your teachers will focus their attention on in the classroom. The lists below show the values of each color teacher.

The Orange Teacher Values:

Spontaneity
Creativity
The unusual and out-of-the-ordinary
Hands-on activities
Concrete materials
Immediate results
Short-term goals
Energy, vitality, movement
Physical activity
Cleverness
Attention
Skills

The Gold Teacher Values:

Student achievement and performance
Proper student behavior
Lack of classroom disruptions

Student punctuality
Classroom rules established and obeyed
Organization and structure
Tradition (the tried and true)
Lecture method of delivering instruction
Subject-oriented classroom activities
Exactness
Hard work
Long-term goals

The Green Teacher Values:

Freedom
Independent thought
Mental activity
Individuality
Ingenuity
Self-control
Competence
Subject- or knowledge-oriented classroom activities
Independent study and projects
Problem-solving approach to instruction
Inquiry and discovery methods of instruction
Future outcomes

The Blue Teacher Values:

Being able to relate to students on a personal level
Giving help to students (academic and social)
A "good feeling tone" in his/her classroom
The esteem of all those in his/her class
Harmony
Understanding
People-oriented concepts and activities
Influencing others for their "good"
Cooperative learning
Imagination and creativity
Success for everyone

Which of the 4 teacher's values match the way you learn best? Why?

____

____

____

____

____

____

Multiple Intelligence

There are many ways besides IQ (intelligence quotient) to measure intellect. Dr. Howard Gardner, a psychologist, has identified seven kinds of intelligence which he calls "multiple intelligences." Another psychologist, Dr. Thomas Armstrong says there are seven kinds of "smarts." These different ways in which people are talented are listed below.

Circle all the ways you think you are smart or intelligent.

1. Musical Intelligence	Music smart
2. Bodily-Kinesthetic Intelligence	Body smart
3. Interpersonal Intelligence	People smart
4. Intrapersonal Intelligence	Self-smart
5.Visual-Spatial Intelligence	Picture smart
6. Linguistic Intelligence	Word smart
7. Logical-Mathematical Intelligence	Logic smart

Dr. Daniel Goleman says we also have an EQ (emotional quotient)—your ability to handle your emotions. He believes it is the most important form of intelligence because it determines how happy and successful you will be.

True Colors and Intelligence

Your True Colors are another method of understanding how you are smart. Each color is intelligent in a different way. Your first color represents your major strengths and your unique kind of smartness.

Below discuss your special talents and which career pathways use your particular kind of smarts. (Your TC cards can be helpful.)

Blue Intelligence

____

____

____

____

____

____

Green Intelligence

____

____

____

____

____

____

Gold Intelligence

Orange Intelligence

True Colors

The Need to Manage Your Weaknesses

The most well-rounded people have developed several parts of their personality—areas that need to be managed in order to be successful. Consider which of the areas above you need to strengthen so that you are more well-rounded in things such as work, finances, and relationships. Since your last color represents your most challenging areas, use the space below to discuss what you need to do to improve in that area.

Example: My last color is gold. I need to work on balancing my checkbook and organizing my desk.

My last color is ______________.

What I need to do to strengthen this area in my life is

____

____

____

____

____

____

____

____

____

____

____

Chapter 8

Research

How to Obtain Information About Career Options

Good decisions cannot be made without information. It is time to gather information about your top career choices in order to decide which will be most fulfilling. In addition to learning the values and skills needed for each option, you will need to know such things as duties, education/training, and salary.

Your school counselor can help you with career information. You may also use any of the following, as well as other resources found in most libraries and career centers, to do your research.

1. The **Dictionary of Occupational Titles (DOT)** lists over 35,000 job titles and more than 20,000 different occupations. A job description is given with skills required for each occupation.

2. The **Occupational Outlook Handbook (OOH)** includes information on job descriptions, places of employment, training, educational requirements, and salary ranges. The salary information is national and, therefore, the estimates will be low for the greater Los Angeles area.

3. The **ONET—Occupational Information Network** is a computer database designed to replace the DOT and OOH.

4. The **Guide for Occupational Exploration (GOE)** is based on worker trait group interests that relate to possible occupations.

5. **Vocational Biographies** tell true stories of workers in over 875 occupations

You may want to check out these career assessment web sites:

1. www.truecolorscareer.com
   This site offers information about the book **Follow Your True Colors to the Work You Love**.

2. www.truecolors.org
   This web site gives an assessment as well as other information about the True Colors program.

3. www.keirsey.com
   This site offers The Keirsey Character Sorter and The Keirsey Temperament Sorter based on the Myers-Briggs personality types.

4. www2.ncsu.edu/unity/lockers/users/l/lkj
   The Career Key offers a free public service to help people make sound career decisions (based on Holland's theory).

5. www.self-directed-search.com
   A career assessment based on the Self-Directed Search ($7.95 as of July 1999).

Career centers usually will have one of the following resourceful systems:

Discover—A complete computer-based career information and planning system. You may go directly to the "information only" file for occupational information.

Eureka—A California career information system that delivers occupational and educational information on 390 occupations, 140 programs of study and training, 221 post-secondary schools in California, and more than 1,700 colleges and universities in the United States.

Career Worksheets

Use the following career research worksheets to answer questions about each of your five or more options.

CAREER RESEARCH WORKSHEET

Position title: ______________________________

Description of duties and responsibilities: ______________________________

____

____

____

Where to look for this type of career: ______________________________

____

____

Education, training, or experience required: ______________________________

____

____

____

Beneficial personal qualities: ______________________________

____

____

Expected earnings: ______________________

Immediate outlook for this career (1-5 years): ______________________

Long-term outlook (5-10 years): ______________________

Sources and references: ______________________

CAREER RESEARCH WORKSHEET

Position title: ____

Description of duties and responsibilities: ___________________________

____

____

____

Where to look for this type of career: ______________________________

____

____

Education, training, or experience required: __________________________

____

____

____

Beneficial personal qualities: ____________________________________

____

____

True Colors

Expected earnings: ____________________

Immediate outlook for this career (1-5 years): ____________________

____

____

____

____

Long-term outlook (5-10 years): ____________________

____

____

____

____

Sources and references: ____________________

____

____

____

____

____

True Colors

CAREER RESEARCH WORKSHEET

Position title: ____

Description of duties and responsibilities: ________________________

____

____

____

Where to look for this type of career: ________________________

____

____

Education, training, or experience required: ____________________

____

____

____

Beneficial personal qualities: ______________________________

____

____

True Colors

Expected earnings: ______________________

Immediate outlook for this career (1-5 years): ______________________

____

____

____

____

Long-term outlook (5-10 years): ______________________________

____

____

____

____

Sources and references: ______________________________

____

____

____

____

____

CAREER RESEARCH WORKSHEET

Position title: ____

Description of duties and responsibilities: ____________________

____

____

____

Where to look for this type of career: _________________________

____

____

Education, training, or experience required: ___________________

____

____

____

Beneficial personal qualities: _________________________________

____

____

True Colors

Expected earnings: ____________________

Immediate outlook for this career (1-5 years): ____________________

____

____

____

____

Long-term outlook (5-10 years): ____________________

____

____

____

____

True Colors

Sources and references: ____________________

____

____

____

____

____

CAREER RESEARCH WORKSHEET

Position title: ______________________________

Description of duties and responsibilities: ______________________________

____

____

____

Where to look for this type of career: ______________________________

____

____

Education, training, or experience required: ______________________________

____

____

____

Beneficial personal qualities: ______________________________

____

____

Expected earnings: ____________________

Immediate outlook for this career (1-5 years): ____________________

____

____

____

____

Long-term outlook (5-10 years): ____________________

____

____

____

____

Sources and references: ____________________

____

____

____

____

____

CAREER RESEARCH WORKSHEET

Position title: ____

Description of duties and responsibilities: ________________________

____

____

____

Where to look for this type of career: ____________________________

____

____

Education, training, or experience required: _______________________

____

____

____

Beneficial personal qualities: __________________________________

____

____

Expected earnings: ______________________

Immediate outlook for this career (1-5 years): ______________________

____

____

____

____

Long-term outlook (5-10 years): ______________________

____

____

____

____

Sources and references: ______________________

____

____

____

____

____

Tying It All Together

The information provided should have given you some options to help make a decision about the direction you want to take in your career. To experience satisfaction in your work, it is important to be who you are by expressing your true values, and do what you love by using your best skills. Your career decision could eventually lead to your life's work—your ultimate career. The exercise below will help you evaluate your choices and clarify their soundness.

Clarifying your Values, Skills, and Occupations

Your values clarify how you need to express yourself in your work. List five or more of your most important values from chapter 3.

1. ______________________

2. ______________________

3. ______________________

4. ______________________

5. ______________________

6. ______________________

7. ______________________

When you are able to use your best skills, you enjoy what you do. List five or more of your most enjoyable skills from chapter 4.

1. ________________________

2. ________________________

3. ________________________

4. ___________________________

5. ___________________________

6. ___________________________

7. ___________________________

List five or more of the top career choices from your completed research sheets.

1. ___________________________

2. ___________________________

3. ___________________________

4. ___________________________

5. ___________________________

6. ___________________________

7. ___________________________

Chapter 9

Decision Making and Goal Setting

Goals are the things that you want to accomplish because they have meaning to you. They should be realistic enough for you to believe they are possible, but at the same time not compromise your dreams. Some goals are short-term while others are long-term. A short-term goal might be to get a good grade in your math class so that you can accomplish a long-term goal of being accepted into a university.

Now that you have gained more knowledge about yourself and what you desire in your life, it is time to make it happen. Only you can take responsibility for your own life and accomplish your goals. It is important to keep a positive mental attitude that says, "Yes, I can." If you believe you can—you can! Of course, the opposite is also true. If you believe you can't—you are also right. It's your choice.

My Most Desirable Career

Take the most desirable choice from your list of five top careers in Chapter 6, and complete the following exercise that includes some of your short-term goals.

Career Choice ____

This career is my first choice because ________________________________

____

____

____

____

____

____

Short Term Goals

Goals that I plan to achieve in the next six months to help accomplish my overall goal are:

1.____

2.____

3.____

4.____

5.____

6.____

7.____

Goals I need to achieve within one year to help accomplish my goal are:

1.____

2.____

3.____

4.____

5.____

6.____

7.____

Action Plan

Five steps I need to take to accomplish these short-term goals:

1.

2.

3.

4.

5.

Personal Goals

While making decisions about the direction you want to take in your life, don't forget to include personal goals. Balance in your personal and professional life is very important. You are not just a human being that has physical needs. You also have mental, emotional and spiritual needs. Make a list of goals that address more of your personal needs.

Example: I will exercise 3 times a week, or I will listen to a motivational tape everyday for inspiration.

1.____

2.____

3.____

4.____

5.____

6.____

7.____

Long-Term Goals (Goals I plan to achieve in 5 to 20 years)

It is also important to set long-term goals—those that take more time to accomplish. The more goals you can set for your life, the more direction you will have. Can you think of other goals you would like to accomplish in . . .

5 Years?

1.____

2.____

3.____

4.____

5.____

10 Years?

1.____

2.____

3.____

4.____

5.____

20 Years?

1.____

2.____

3.____

4.____

5.____

Action Plan

Five steps I need to take to accomplish my long-term goals.

1.____

2.____

3.____

4.____

5.____

My True Colors Career Summary

Name ________________________________

My color spectrum: ________ ________ ________ ________

My 5 most important work values

1.____________________________

2.____________________________

3.____________________________

4.____________________________

5.____________________________

My five most enjoyable transferable skills

1.________________________________

2.________________________________

3.________________________________

4.________________________________

5.________________________________

My 3 best learning styles

1.________________________________

2.________________________________

3.________________________________

My list of strongest career options

1.________________________________

2.________________________________

3.________________________________

4.________________________________

5.________________________________

My most desirable career is ____________________.

My short-term goals

1.____________________

2.____________________

3.____________________

4.____________________

5.____________________

My action plan

1.____________________

2.____________________

3.____________________

4.____________________

5.____________________

My personal goals

1.____________________

2.____________________

3.____________________

My long-term goals

1.____________________

2.____________________

3.____________________

4.____________________

5.____________________

My action plan

1.____________________

2.____________________

3.____________________

4.____________________

5.____________________

Also available from True Colors:

Follow Your True Colors to the Work You Love: The Workbook

ISBN 1-893320-20-0

This innovative course in career planning is a must read for college students. Author Carolyn Kalil, a gifted educator, career counselor and speaker, introduces students to the True Colors personality system to help them better understand their natural strengths and talents. Gradually they become equipped to identify careers in which they will thrive and find true satisfaction—work they will love! A terrific resource for any career counselor. 231 pages.

TCP-218-2 . . . . $24.95*
TCP-218-A (Reference Book). $16.95*
TCP-218-IG (Instructor's Guide) $85.00*

Showing Our True Colors

ISBN 1-893320-23-5

Filled with easy-to-use tools for personal growth, this delightfully illustrated book by communication expert Mary Miscisin uncovers the power of the True Colors process. You will discover the characteristics behind each of the four True Colors, as well as tips for understanding, appreciating, and relating to each Color style. Its simple format, charming anecdotes, and convenient reference lists make **Showing Our True Colors** a fun and easy read. And the end result will be a celebration of the uniqueness in yourself and others. 200 plus pages.

TCB-020. . . . . $19.95*

Dare to Dream

ISBN 1-893320-21-9

Super Bowl champ Curt Marsh challenges readers to dig deep and pursue their dreams, whatever their circumstances. Curt talks about the physical and emotional pain he endured when a football injury led to the amputation of his right foot and ankle. And he shares many of the life lessons that have inspired him to rise above his challenges and pursue his passions—including the True Colors process. **Dare to Dream** will inspire you to embrace change and diversity, discover true toughness, set goals and develop plans to achieve them, and much more! 122 pages.

TCB-010. . . . . $19.95*

* Plus shipping and handling

More creative resources from True Colors . . .

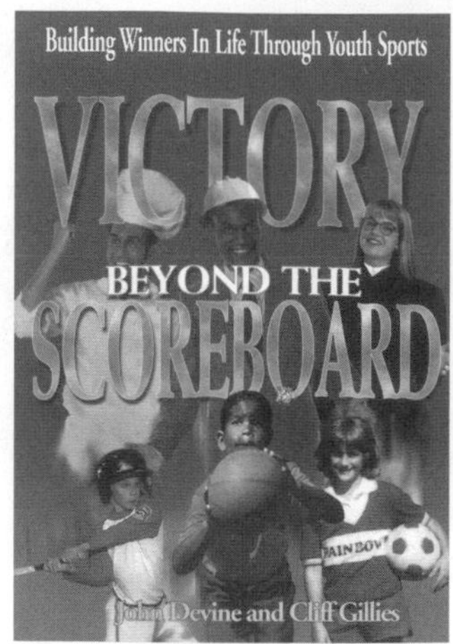

Victory Beyond the Scoreboard

ISBN 1-885221-43-6

At last comes a practical guide with intelligent answers to the social, ethical, and behavioral concerns surrounding youth sports. Chock-full of innovative ideas for making sports more fun and less stressful for children and their families, **Victory Beyond the Scoreboard** clearly outlines how to create a winning partnership among players, parents, and coaches. Authors Cliff Gillies, an award-winning high school principal and coach, and John Devine, a veteran coach of 20 years, have teamed up to offer this "play book" for guiding young athletes. Includes tips for selecting the right sport and program, helping children deal with athletic successes and failures, using sports as a catalyst for family-building, and more! 272 pages.

TCB-060. . . . . $14.95*

The Sports Management Journal

ISBN 1-885221-97-5

The Sports Management Journal is an easy-to-use workbook written specifically for school coaches and parents of children in sports. In this wonderful companion to **Victory Beyond the Scoreboard**, author Cliff Gillies presents tear-out exercises to copy and use in daily coaching and parenting. You'll also find a proven design for coach-parent teaming, games for teaching respectful communication, charts for athletic achievement and improvement, the True Colors personality assessment system and cards, and much more! 179 pages.

TCB-061. . . . . $14.95*

Action &Communication Guide

Our popular **Action & Communication Guide** will help identify the "personality" of your classroom and provide effective ways to help you better relate to each student. Features a durable binder and four "colorized" sections—one for each personality type. 88 pages chock full of valuable insight for creating a stimulating classroom environment, motivating learning and achievement, gaining cooperation and more!

TCP230 . . . . $34.95*
TCP225-C (Without binder). $29.95*

* Plus shipping and handling

True Colors, Inc., 12395 Doherty Street, Riverside, California 92503 · Telephone: (800) 422-4686 or (909) 371-3901
Facsimile (909) 371-1701 · E-Mail: info@truecolors.org · Web Site: www.truecolors.org